ITALY

WORLD ADVENTURES

BY STEFFI CAVELL-CLARKE

BookLife

©2018
Book Life
King's Lynn
Norfolk PE30 4LS

ISBN: 978-1-78637-241-3

Written by:
Steffi Cavell–Clarke

Edited by:
Kirsty Holmes

Designed by:
Dan Scase

A catalogue record for this book
is available from the British Library.

 Library 3/18  Cheshire East Council

www.cheshireeast.gov.uk/libraries

Please return this book on or before the date it is due back. The date will be shown on your self-service receipt or below. To keep your books for longer, please renew online, call the renewal line 0300 1237739 or visit a library.

Ellesmere Port
Library
0151 337 4684/5
Monday
Thursday &
Friday 9-7
Tuesday &
Wednesday 9-5
Saturday 9-1

 Libraries 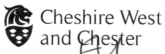 Cheshire West and Chester

www.cheshirewestandchester.gov.uk/libraries

ITALY
WORLD ADVENTURES

CONTENTS

Words in **red** can be found in the glossary on page 24.

3

WHERE IS ITALY?

Italy is a country in the southern part of Europe. The capital city of Italy is called Rome.

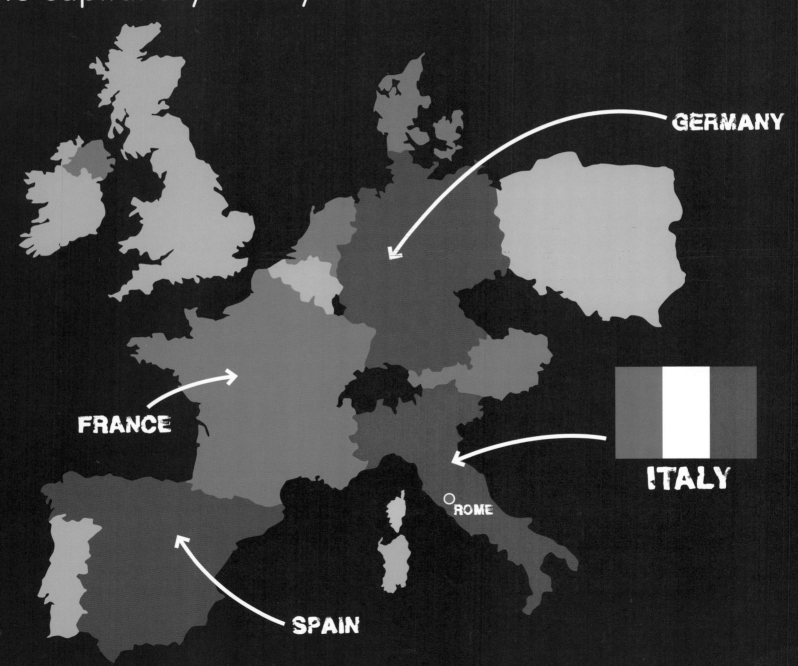

GERMANY

FRANCE

ITALY

ROME

SPAIN

The **population** of Italy is over 61 million.
Millions of people live in the big cities of Italy.
The main language spoken in Italy is Italian.

WEATHER AND LANDSCAPE

The weather in Italy changes with the seasons.
It has hot, dry summers and cool, wet winters.

Italy has many different landscapes. It has snowy mountain peaks, large lakes, flat **plains** and long, sandy **coastal areas**.

The highest peak between France and Italy is Monte Bianco, which is 4,807 metres high.

CLOTHING

People in Italy mostly wear **modern** and comfortable clothing because of the warm weather.

Italy is famous for its fashion and style.

There are different types of **traditional** clothes
in Italy that are worn during special celebrations.
These colourful **embroidered** skirts and hats are
decorated with flowers or fruit.

RELIGION

There are many different **religions** that people follow. The religion with the most followers in Italy is Christianity.

Most Christians in Italy
are **Roman Catholic,**
and **worship** in a church.

**A Roman
Catholic
Cathedral in
Rome, Italy**

FOOD

SPAGHETTI
BOLOGNESE

Italy is famous for its pasta dishes. Pasta is made from flour, eggs, salt and water. Spaghetti Bolognese is a traditional dish that is now eaten all around the world.

Pizza was invented in Naples, Italy. It is usually baked in a wood-fired oven and covered with fresh tomatoes and mozzarella cheese.

AT SCHOOL

In Italy, most children go to school between the ages of 6 and 16. Some children learn at home. They all study Italian, English, maths, science and history.

Many children in Italy go to after-school clubs where they can play games and sports, like football.

AT HOME

Many people in Italy live in towns and cities, such as Florence and Milan. These people often live in modern flats.

Many people also live on farms. Farms in Italy grow lots of crops, such as tomatoes, grapes and olives.

FAMILIES

Most children live with their parents, **siblings** or other family members like grandparents.

Families in Italy like to get together for special occasions, such as weddings and religious holidays.

SPORT

These fans are supporting the Italian football team.

One of the most popular sports in Italy is football. Italy has won the World Cup four times.

Other sports, such as basketball, tennis, skiing and cycling are also very popular in Italy.

FUN FACTS

Vatican City is the smallest country in the world and it is found inside Italy.

It is the home of the Pope.

It has its own phone lines, radio, T.V. stations, money and stamps. It even has its own army called the Swiss Guard.

Rome was home to the ancient Romans.
The ancient Romans built the Colosseum in
Rome, where they would watch hunting games.

COLOSSEUM

GLOSSARY

cathedral	a large building used for Christian worship
coastal areas	land near to the coast
embroidered	material that has a raised pattern sewn into it
modern	something from present or recent times
plains	large areas of flat land with few trees
population	number of people living in a place
religions	belief in a god or gods
Roman Catholic	a member of the Roman Catholic church
siblings	brothers and sisters
traditional	ways of behaving that have been done for a long time
worship	a religions act, such as praying

INDEX

Photocredits: Abbreviations: l–left, r–right, b–bottom, t–top, c–centre, m–middle.

Front Cover – Svitlana–ua, bg – Aleksey Klints. 1 – Aleksey Klints. 2 – Istvan Csak. 3 – Svitlana–ua. 5 – Luciano Mortula – LGM. 6 – ronnybas. 7 – Nando Machado. 8 – Sanneberg. 9 – Hibiscus81. 10 – Luis Enrique Torres. 11 – Lisa S. 12 – Karpenkov Denis. 13 – Lestertair. 14 – LuckyImages. 15 – matimix. 16 – RossHelen. 17 – Lukasz Szwaj. 18 – Iakov Filimonov. 19 – oliveromg. 20 – Juri Pozzi. 21 – Lukas Gojda. 22tl – S.Borisov. 22m – giulio napolitano. 22br – Ugis Riba. 23br – Marco Rubino. Images are courtesy of Shutterstock.com. With thanks to Getty Images, Thinkstock Photo and iStockphoto.